EASY FRENCH FRIES COOKBOOK

RE-IMAGINE FRENCH FRIES WITH 50 DELICIOUS FRENCH FRY RECIPES

By
BookSumo Press

Published by
http://www.booksumo.com/

ABOUT THE AUTHOR.

BookSumo Press is a publisher of unique, easy, and healthy cookbooks.

Our cookbooks span all topics and all subjects. If you want a deep dive into the possibilities of cooking with any type of ingredient. Then BookSumo Press is your go to place for robust yet simple and delicious cookbooks and recipes. Whether you are looking for great tasting pressure cooker recipes or authentic ethic and cultural food. BookSumo Press has a delicious and easy cookbook for you.

With simple ingredients, and even simpler step-by-step instructions BookSumo cookbooks get everyone in the kitchen chefing delicious meals.

BookSumo is an independent publisher of books operating in the beautiful Garden State (NJ) and our team of chefs and kitchen experts are here to teach, eat, and be merry!

INTRODUCTION

Welcome to *The Effortless Chef Series*! Thank you for taking the time to purchase this cookbook.

Come take a journey into the delights of easy cooking. The point of this cookbook and all BookSumo Press cookbooks is to exemplify the effortless nature of cooking simply.

In this book we focus on French Fries. You will find that even though the recipes are simple, the taste of the dishes are quite amazing.

So will you take an adventure in simple cooking? If the answer is yes please consult the table of contents to find the dishes you are most interested in.

Once you are ready, jump right in and start cooking.

— BookSumo Press

TABLE OF CONTENTS

ANY ISSUES? CONTACT US

If you find that something important to you is missing from this book please contact us at info@booksumo.com.

We will take your concerns into consideration when the 2nd edition of this book is published. And we will keep you updated!

— BookSumo Press

LEGAL NOTES

COMMON ABBREVIATIONS

cup(s)	C.
tablespoon	tbsp
teaspoon	tsp
ounce	oz.
pound	lb

*All units used are standard American measurements

Chapter 1: Easy French Fries Recipes

How to Make an American French Fry

INGREDIENTS

- 4 -5 large russet potatoes, skin removed, cut into thin strips, soaked in cold water
- peanut oil
- kosher salt

Directions

- Set your oven to 200 degrees before doing anything else.
- At the same time begin to get some peanut oil hot in a Dutch oven. Heat the oil until it reaches a temperature of 330 degrees F.
- Drain your potatoes from the cold water they were soaked in as you cut them and pat them dry.
- Once you oil has reached the ideal temperature place your fries into the oil carefully. Working in sets cook your potatoes for 4 mins then place them on a paper towel lined plate.
- Once all the potatoes have cooked for 4 mins and drained from excess oils. Get your oil hotter to 375 degrees.
- Once the oil has reached the new temperature begin to refry the potatoes for another 4 mins until they are crispy.
- Place everything on a rack for draining then once all the potatoes have been refried and drained coat them with salt.
- Enjoy.

Amount per serving: 4

Timing Information:

Preparation	10 mins
Total Time	55 mins

Nutritional Information:

Calories	284.1
Fat	0.3g
Cholesterol	0.0mg
Sodium	22.1mg
Carbohydrates	64.4g
Protein	7.4g

* Percent Daily Values are based on a 2,000 calorie diet.

SEASONED FRIES WITH FLASH FREEZING

In this recipe we flash freeze our fries after cooking them. There are two benefits to flash freezing 1. Our fries will last a long time in the freezer frozen and 2. Cooking the fries then freezing them and re cooking them will increase the flavor.

INGREDIENTS

- potato, skin removed, cut into strips
- olive oil
- creole seasoning, see appendix

Directions

- Set your oven to 425 degrees before doing anything else.
- Get a resealable plastic bag and place your cut potatoes into the plastic bag. Pour in some olive oil and also some creole seasoning liberally.
- Shake your potatoes in the bag to evenly coat them with oil and spices.
- Lay out all your potatoes in a casserole dish. Once all the potatoes have been laid into the dish and oven has reached its proper temperature. Bake the fries in the oven for about 20 to 30 mins until they are just completely cooked.
- Let the fries and dish lose their heat and reach room temperature then place all the fries and the dish itself into the freezer to flash freeze your fries.
- Once everything is frozen remove the fries from the freezer and carefully place everything into resealable bags for storage or large Tupperware.
- When you like some fries, remove a serving from the freezer and reheat them in the oven at 425 degrees for about 17 mins.
- Enjoy.

Amount per serving: 1

Timing Information:

| Preparation | 15 mins |
| Total Time | 45 mins |

Nutritional Information:

Calories	0.0
Fat	0.0g
Cholesterol	0.0mg
Sodium	0.0mg
Carbohydrates	0.0g
Protein	0.0g

* Percent Daily Values are based on a 2,000 calorie diet.

GARLIC FESTIVAL FRIES

INGREDIENTS

- 1 32 ounce bags frozen French fries
- 3 teaspoons peanut oil
- 3/4 teaspoon salt
- cooking spray
- 2 tablespoons butter
- 8 garlic cloves, minced
- 2 tablespoons fresh parsley, finely chopped
- 2 tablespoons parmesan cheese

Directions

- Set your oven to 400 degrees before doing anything else.
- Get a resealable bag and place the fries in the bag along with the oil and salt. Shake the bag to evenly coat the fries with oil and salt.
- Place all your fries on a baking dish that has been coated with nonstick spray. Evenly space out the potatoes on the dish and cook everything for 12 mins then flip the fries and continue to cook them for another 10 mins.
- Now get a frying pan and begin to heat it add in your garlic and butter and cook the garlic for 3 mins with a low level of heat. Whisk the garlic as it cooks to avoid burning and to season the butter. Add in your cheese, parsley, and potatoes into the pan and continue to cook and stir everything for about 2 more mins.
- Try to get all the fries evenly coated with butter and spice.
- Enjoy.

Amount per serving: 6

Timing Information:

Preparation	5 mins
Total Time	55 mins

Nutritional Information:

Calories	289.5
Fat	13.6g
Cholesterol	11.6mg
Sodium	853.0mg
Carbohydrates	38.9g
Protein	4.3g

* Percent Daily Values are based on a 2,000 calorie diet.

RING ONIONS FRIED FRENCH

Frying times for these French fried onion rings varies on the temperature of your oil. A general estimate is about 3-5 mins per side should be sufficient. But this could be shorter or longer depending on temperatures. So keep an eye on them.

INGREDIENTS

- 3 large onions, sliced into thin rings
- 2 cups milk
- 2 cups all-purpose flour, in a bowl
- oil
- salt

Directions

- Place your milk in a bowl and submerge your onions in the milk. Leave the onions to sit in the milk for 8 mins.
- As the onions are soaking add oil to a Dutch oven and begin to get it hot for frying.
- Once the oil is hot submerge a batch of soaked onions into the flour and coat them evenly with flour. Once the onions have been coated evenly and the oil is hot begin to fry the onions in batches in the oil until they are brown and golden.
- Place the fried rings on a paper towel lined plate to drain then coat them with some salt. Enjoy.

Amount per serving: 1

Timing Information:

Preparation	15 mins
Total Time	45 mins

Nutritional Information:

Calories	280.4
Fat	4.1g
Cholesterol	13.6mg
Sodium	52.4mg
Carbohydrates	51.1g
Protein	9.3g

* Percent Daily Values are based on a 2,000 calorie diet.

ITALIAN COUNTRYSIDE FRIES

INGREDIENTS

- 6 medium potatoes, skin removed, sliced into fries
- 1 ounce Italian dressing
- 2 tablespoons oil
- 1 tablespoon fresh parsley, Chopped

Directions

- Set your oven to 350 degrees before doing anything else.
- Once your potatoes have been sliced pat them dry and let them sit for about 20 mins to dry out further.
- Get a bowl and place your fries in it. Top the fries with the oil and stir everything.
- Get a cookie sheet or casserole dish and place your fries into the dish or on the sheet. Top the fries evenly with the dressing mix and then toss everything. Then top the fries again with the parsley and toss again.
- Cook the fries in the oven for 22 mins then turn the fries over.
- Now continue to cook then for 4 to 8 more mins with an oven temperature of 450.
- Enjoy.

Amount per serving: 4

Timing Information:

Preparation	20 mins
Total Time	55 mins

Nutritional Information:

Calories	306.4
Fat	7.1g
Cholesterol	0.0mg
Sodium	19.7mg
Carbohydrates	55.8g
Protein	6.4g

* Percent Daily Values are based on a 2,000 calorie diet.

TWO TIMES ROASTED FRIES

INGREDIENTS

- 4 russet potatoes, peeled and cut into French fry strips.
- 1/2 cup butter, melted
- salt and pepper
- garlic powder
- onion powder
- 1 dash cayenne pepper

Directions

- Set your oven to 375 degrees before doing anything else.
- Coat a casserole dish with cooking spray and then place your fries on the dish and cook them in the hot oven for 13 mins.
- Remove the fries from the oven top them with the melted butter. Top the fries with some pepper and salt onion and garlic powder, and cayenne Toss everything to evenly coat the fries then place everything back in the oven for about 10 to 12 more mins or until they are done to your liking.
- Enjoy.

Amount per serving: 4

Timing Information:

Preparation	15 mins
Total Time	40 mins

Nutritional Information:

Calories	265.8
Fat	11.7g
Cholesterol	30.5mg
Sodium	94.5mg
Carbohydrates	37.2g
Protein	4.4g

* Percent Daily Values are based on a 2,000 calorie diet.

SPICY SWEET-POTATO FRIES

INGREDIENTS

- 1 large egg white
- 2 teaspoons chili powder
- 1/2 teaspoon salt
- 1/4 teaspoon garlic powder
- 1/4 teaspoon onion powder
- 16 ounces pared sweet potatoes, cut into 1/2 inch strips

Directions

- Set your oven to 450 degrees before doing anything else.
- Get a bowl, combine: spices and eggs. Beat the mix completely then combine in the potatoes and toss everything to coat the fries nicely.
- Lay out all your potatoes in a casserole dish and cook them for about 11 mins in the oven. Then flip the fries and continue baking for 11 more mins.
- Enjoy.

Amount per serving: 4

Timing Information:

Preparation	10 mins
Total Time	30 mins

Nutritional Information:

Calories	106.7
Fat	0.2g
Cholesterol	0.0mg
Sodium	389.1mg
Carbohydrates	23.8g
Protein	2.9g

* Percent Daily Values are based on a 2,000 calorie diet.

NO FRY FRIES

INGREDIENTS

- 5 large baking potatoes, cut into matchsticks
- light vegetable oil cooking spray
- 2 large egg whites
- 1 tablespoon Cajun spices

Directions

- Set your oven 400 degrees before doing anything else.
- Get a casserole dish and coat it with non-stick spray.
- Get a bowl for your egg whites, and begin to beat them with the Cajun spice. Combine in the potatoes and toss everything evenly.
- Lay out your coated potatoes in the casserole dish and spread them evenly with space and cook then in the oven on the lowest rack for a time of around 40 mins.
- Try to flip your potatoes every 7 to 10 mins.
- Enjoy.

Amount per serving: 4

Timing Information:

Preparation	20 mins
Total Time	1 hr 5 mins

Nutritional Information:

Calories	171.2
Fat	0.2g
Cholesterol	0.0mg
Sodium	34.8mg
Carbohydrates	37.7g
Protein	5.3g

* Percent Daily Values are based on a 2,000 calorie diet.

A 4ᵀᴴ Grader's Lunch

INGREDIENTS

- 4 sweet potatoes, skin removed, cut into strips
- canola oil for deep frying
- salt

Directions

- Get your oil hot in a Dutch oven about 350 degrees.
- Once the oil is hot, place your potatoes in a bowl and coat them with some salt and toss everything.
- Begin to fry the potatoes in batches, then place them on a paper towel lined plate to drain. Fry the potatoes for about 3 mins each side or until crispy.
- Continue for the remaining fries. Let everything drain on the paper towel line plate.
- Enjoy.

Amount per serving: 4

Timing Information:

Preparation	5 mins
Total Time	35 mins

Nutritional Information:

Calories	111.8
Fat	0.0g
Cholesterol	0.0mg
Sodium	71.5mg
Carbohydrates	26.1g
Protein	2.0g

* Percent Daily Values are based on a 2,000 calorie diet.

UPPER VENICE FRIES

INGREDIENTS

- 5 medium potatoes, scrubbed, cut into wedges
- 1/2 cup light Italian dressing
- 3 tablespoons olive oil

Directions

- Set your oven to 350 degrees before doing anything else.
- Place you potato wedges into a bowl and toss them with the Italian dressing.
- Get a casserole dish and coat it liberally with olive oil then place in your wedges and toss them in the oil evenly.
- Cook everything in the oven for about 50 to 55 mins. Check and flip your potatoes every 10 mins.
- Enjoy.

Amount per serving: 4

Timing Information:

Preparation	10 mins
Total Time	55 mins

Nutritional Information:

Calories	317.0
Fat	12.2g
Cholesterol	1.8mg
Sodium	338.3mg
Carbohydrates	47.8g
Protein	5.5g

* Percent Daily Values are based on a 2,000 calorie diet.

MEDITERRANEAN SEA FRENCH FRIES

INGREDIENTS

- 3 lbs russet potatoes, peeled and cut into thick matchsticks
- 1/4-1/2 cup Extra Virgin olive oil
- nonstick spray
- salt
- 1 lemon, to serve

Directions

- Set your oven to 400 degrees before doing anything else.
- Get a bowl and place your potatoes in it. Coat the potatoes with the oil and toss everything to coat them evenly.
- Get a casserole dish and coat it with some nonstick spray then some olive oil. Evenly space out your potatoes and cook them in the oven for 55 mins and flip them half way.
- Once the potatoes are done baking coat them with some salt to your liking. Then squeeze the lemon juice over them evenly.
- Enjoy.

Amount per serving: 6

Timing Information:

Preparation	10 mins
Total Time	1 hr

Nutritional Information:

Calories	257.9
Fat	9.2g
Cholesterol	0.0mg
Sodium	14.3mg
Carbohydrates	41.5g
Protein	4.8g

* Percent Daily Values are based on a 2,000 calorie diet.

2-Ingredient Mexican Fries

INGREDIENTS

- 2 tablespoons taco seasoning
- 1 26 ounce bags frozen crispy French fries

Directions

- Place your potatoes in a casserole dish that has been coated with nonstick spray. Place your potatoes in the dish and cook them in the oven at about 425 degrees until they are golden brown and done about 22 to 25 mins.
- Place your baked fries into a bowl and toss them with the taco seasoning evenly.
- Enjoy.

Amount per serving: 6

Timing Information:

Preparation	0 mins
Total Time	15 mins

Nutritional Information:

Calories	188.3
Fat	4.6g
Cholesterol	0.0mg
Sodium	529.4mg
Carbohydrates	33.6g
Protein	3.1g

* Percent Daily Values are based on a 2,000 calorie diet.

FRENCH FRIES FROM BELGIUM

INGREDIENTS

- 2 lbs potato, peeled, chopped into matchsticks
- 2 tsps Herbes de Provence, see appendix
- salt
- oil for deep frying
- mayo, as dip for serving

Directions

- Get you oil hot to 300 degrees F. Then once the oil is hot begin to fry your French fries in batches for 7 mins. Then remove them from the oil carefully and let them drain on a paper towel lined plate. Once all the fries have been preliminary cooked increase the heat of the oil to 350 degrees F. Once the oil is hot at the new temperature.
- Begin to fry them again for 6 more mins.
- Top the fries with some salt and the Herbes de Provence. Place some mayo on to the side as a dip for the fries.
- Enjoy.

Amount per serving: 6

Timing Information:

Preparation	20 mins
Total Time	30 mins

Nutritional Information:

Calories	128.3
Fat	0.1g
Cholesterol	0.0mg
Sodium	10.0mg
Carbohydrates	29.1g
Protein	3.3g

* Percent Daily Values are based on a 2,000 calorie diet.

Low-Fat Almost No Fat Fries

INGREDIENTS

- 4 -6 potatoes, cut into wedges
- cooking spray
- salt and pepper

Directions

- Set your oven to 350 degrees before doing anything else.
- Coat a casserole dish with nonstick soybean oil spray. Then place your wedges in the dish. Spray the potatoes with some more spray then top everything with a bit of pepper and some salt. Toss the potatoes then cook everything in the oven for 32 mins.
- Enjoy.

Amount per serving: 2

Timing Information:

Preparation	5 mins
Total Time	35 mins

Nutritional Information:

Calories	328.0
Fat	0.3g
Cholesterol	0.0mg
Sodium	25.5mg
Carbohydrates	74.4g
Protein	8.6g

* Percent Daily Values are based on a 2,000 calorie diet.

FRENCH FRIES FOR JULY

INGREDIENTS

- 2 egg whites
- 1/2 teaspoon chili powder
- 3/4 teaspoon ground cumin
- 1/4 teaspoon black pepper
- 1/2 teaspoon table salt
- 2 large potatoes, scrubbed, chopped into thick matchsticks

Directions

- Coat a baking dish with nonstick spray then set your oven to 425 degrees before doing anything else.
- Get a bowl, combine: egg whites, cumin, chili powder, pepper, salt, and potatoes. Toss everything evenly. Then place the potatoes into the baking dish evenly. Cook everything in the oven for 17 mins. Then set the oven to broiler.
- Do not broil the potatoes just keep them cooking for about 5 to 9 more mins.
- Enjoy.

Amount per serving: 4

Timing Information:

Preparation	10 mins
Total Time	35 mins

Nutritional Information:

Calories	153.4
Fat	0.3g
Cholesterol	0.0mg
Sodium	335.3mg
Carbohydrates	32.7g
Protein	5.6g

* Percent Daily Values are based on a 2,000 calorie diet.

HOT PEPPER WHITE PEPPER FRENCH FRIES

INGREDIENTS

- 4 large potatoes, scrubbed, cut into strips
- 8 cups ice water
- 1 teaspoon garlic powder
- 1 teaspoon onion powder
- 1/4 teaspoon salt
- 1 teaspoon white pepper
- 1/4 teaspoon allspice
- 1 teaspoon hot pepper flakes
- 1 tablespoon vegetable oil

Directions

- Get a bowl of cold water with some ice and submerge your potatoes in it. Place a covering of plastic on the bowl, and let the potatoes sit in the water for 2 hours.
- Drain the potatoes from the water and pat them dry let them sit for about 15 to 20 mins.Set your oven to 475 degrees before doing anything else.
- Get a resealable plastic bag and add in the following spices then toss them together: pepper flakes, garlic and onion powder, allspice, salt, and white pepper. Once the spices have been tossed together evenly.
- Add in your potatoes and toss everything. Coat your potatoes with some oil then place everything into a casserole dish that has been coated with nonstick spray.
- Cover the dish with some foil and cook the potatoes for 17 mins in the oven. Discard the foil and continue to bake the fires for another 12 to 15 mins or until they are fully done.
- Try to flip the fries at least twice during the baking process when there is no foil on the dish.
- Enjoy.

Amount per serving: 5

Timing Information:

Preparation	5 mins
Total Time	20 mins

Nutritional Information:

Calories	257.2
Fat	3.0g
Cholesterol	0.0mg
Sodium	136.3mg
Carbohydrates	52.9g
Protein	6.1g

* Percent Daily Values are based on a 2,000 calorie diet.

ENGLISH SALTY VINEGAR FRIES

INGREDIENTS

- 1 1/4 lbs baking potatoes, scrubbed, peeled, chopped into thin fries
- 3 cups water
- 2 tablespoons distilled white vinegar, plus
- 2 teaspoons distilled white vinegar, divided
- 1 tablespoon canola oil
- salt

Directions

- Get a bowl and combine your 2 tbsp of white vinegar and the water. Stir the liquid then place your potatoes in it. Let the potatoes sit under water for at least 40 mins to 45 mins.
- Now set your oven to 400 degrees before doing anything else.
- Once the oven is hot drain your potatoes and pat them dry.
- Get a 2nd bowl for your potatoes after they have been patted dry. Add in your canola oil to the bowl and stir the potatoes to evenly coat them.
- Get a casserole dish or jelly roll pan and coat it with some nonstick spray. Evenly spread out your potatoes on the dish and once the oven is hot begin to cook them for 22 mins. Flip the potatoes by stirring everything and continue to bake them for about 7 to 11 more mins or until you find that they are completely done.
- Remove the fries from the oven and let them cool slightly then mix the fries with two more tsps of vinegar and liberally with some salt according to your tastes.
- Enjoy.

Amount per serving: 4

Timing Information:

Preparation	5 mins
Total Time	20 mins

Nutritional Information:

Calories	156.1
Fat	3.6g
Cholesterol	0.0mg
Sodium	11.2mg
Carbohydrates	28.5g
Protein	2.6g

* Percent Daily Values are based on a 2,000 calorie diet.

3-INGREDIENT FRENCH FRIES

INGREDIENTS

- 2 russet potatoes, cut into fries
- 2 tablespoons olive oil
- 2 tablespoons approximate sodium-free seasoning anything without salt

Directions

- Set your oven to 350 degrees before doing anything else.
- Place your fries into a bowl, and toss them with the olive oil. Once the potatoes have been evenly coated place them on a jelly roll pan evenly. Coat the pan with some nonstick spray. Top your fires with the 2 tbsps of seasoning and toss them well.
- Cook the fries in the oven for about 35 to 45 mins. Flip them after about 25 to 30 mins.
- Enjoy.

Amount per serving: 2

Timing Information:

Preparation	8 mins
Total Time	53 mins

Nutritional Information:

Calories	283.3
Fat	13.6g
Cholesterol	0.0mg
Sodium	13.0mg
Carbohydrates	37.2g
Protein	4.3g

* Percent Daily Values are based on a 2,000 calorie diet.

4-INGREDIENT CLASSICALS

INGREDIENTS

- 2 large potatoes, peeled, cut into matchsticks
- 1/4 teaspoon salt
- oil for frying
- 1/4 cup of melted buttter

Directions

- Get a bowl of water with ice. Place you cut potatoes into the bowl and let them sit submerged for 60 to 80 mins.
- Drain all the excess liquid and begin to get your oil hot to 325 degrees. Working in sets fry your potatoes for 7 mins. Place the potatoes on a paper towel line plate to drain. Once the potatoes have dried a bit top them with the salt evenly, then the butter and toss everything together.
- Enjoy.

Amount per serving: 1

Timing Information:

Preparation	10 mins
Total Time	20 mins

Nutritional Information:

Calories	584.1
Fat	8.3g
Cholesterol	15mg
Sodium	512.8mg
Carbohydrates	64.4g
Protein	7.4g

* Percent Daily Values are based on a 2,000 calorie diet.

Parmesan Onions and Fries

INGREDIENTS

- 3 medium potatoes, sliced into thinner wedges
- 3 tablespoons butter or 3 tablespoons vegetable oil
- 1 -2 tablespoon hot sauce, at room temperature
- 2 cups French's French fried onions, finely crushed
- 1/2 cup parmesan cheese, grated
- 1 C. ketchup, optional

Directions

- Set your oven to 400 degrees before doing anything else.
- Get a bowl, place your hot sauce, butter, and fries into the bowl and toss them evenly.
- Get a 2nd bowl, combine your cheese and fried onions and work the mix evenly.
- Coat your potatoes with the onion mix evenly by pressing the wedges into the mix then place everything into a casserole dish that has been coated with nonstick spray.
- Cook everthing in the oven for 24 mins then once the potatoes are done take them out the oven to cool.
- Get a small bowl combine your ketchup and 2 tbsps of hot and stir everything together.
- Top your fries with the ketchup sauce and toss them evenly.
- Enjoy.

Amount per serving: 4

Timing Information:

Preparation	10 mins
Total Time	35 mins

Nutritional Information:

Calories	253.6
Fat	0.3g
Cholesterol	0.0mg
Sodium	312.8mg
Carbohydrates	64.4g
Protein	7.4g

* Percent Daily Values are based on a 2,000 calorie diet.

SEASONED CRINKLE CUTS

INGREDIENTS

- 5 cups frozen crinkle cut French fries
- 1 teaspoon onion salt
- 1/4 teaspoon paprika
- 1/3 cup grated parmesan cheese

Directions

- Set your oven to 450 degrees before doing anything else.
- Get a casserole dish and coat it with nonstick spray. Place your fries in the dish and top them with the paprika and onion salt.
- Toss everything evenly to coat the fries nicely.
- Cook your fries in the oven for about 17 mins to 22 mins or until completely done. Once the fries are finished top them with the parmesan cheese.
- Enjoy.

Amount per serving: 4

Timing Information:

Preparation	5 mins
Total Time	20 mins

Nutritional Information:

Calories	36.2
Fat	2.4g
Cholesterol	7.3mg
Sodium	127.3mg
Carbohydrates	0.4g
Protein	3.2g

* Percent Daily Values are based on a 2,000 calorie diet.

ATHENIAN YUKON FRIES

INGREDIENTS

- 4 Yukon gold potatoes, sliced matchsticks
- 2 -3 cups extra virgin olive oil
- salt
- oregano
- grated Parmigiano-Reggiano cheese or pecorino Romano cheese
- 1/8-1/4 fluid ounce lemon juice

Directions

- Get your olive oil hot in a frying pan. Working in sets begin to fry your potatoes in the oil until they are golden. Place them on a paper towel lined plate to drain.
- Once all the potatoes have been fried and drained top them with oregano, pepper and salt. Toss everything evenly, then top the fries with the cheese of your choice.
- Toss the fries again then top everything with the lemon juice and toss one final time before serving.
- Enjoy.

Amount per serving: 2

Timing Information:

Preparation	10 mins
Total Time	25 mins

Nutritional Information:

Calories	2146.5
Fat	216.2g
Cholesterol	0.0mg
Sodium	15.2mg
Carbohydrates	54.9g
Protein	5.0g

* Percent Daily Values are based on a 2,000 calorie diet.

Fry 'Em Twice Fries

INGREDIENTS

- water about 4 quarts water
- 1/4 cup white sugar
- 6 large red potatoes cut into 1/4 to 1/3-inch strips
- canola oil or use vegetable oil, use enough oil to cover potatoes completely
- seasoning salt

Directions

- Get a bowl, combine your water and sugar. Place your potatoes into the water and let them sit in the fridge for 7 hours. Remove the fries from the fridge and dry them.
- Now begin to get your oil hot 375 degrees in a Dutch oven then once the oil is hot being to fry you potatoes in set. Let the fries cook for about 7 to 9 mins then remove the fries from the oil and begin with next set.
- Continue frying your potatoes in sets until everything has been cooked in the oil. Place the potatoes on a paper towel lined plate then all your salt to the potatoes as soon as they have been removed from the oil to the plate.
- Enjoy.

Amount per serving: 8

Timing Information:

Preparation	24 hrs
Total Time	24 hrs 6 mins

Nutritional Information:

Calories	217.9
Fat	0.3g
Cholesterol	0.0mg
Sodium	49.8mg
Carbohydrates	50.2g
Protein	5.2g

* Percent Daily Values are based on a 2,000 calorie diet.

GEORGIA BACKROAD FRIES

INGREDIENTS

- 1 1/2 cups all-purpose flour
- 1 1/2 teaspoons paprika
- 1 teaspoon salt
- 1/2 teaspoon ground black pepper
- 1/2 teaspoon chili powder
- 1/4 teaspoon cayenne pepper
- 1 egg
- 1/3 cup milk
- 6 potatoes, cut into wedges
- 1/4 cup vegetable oil

Directions

- Coat a jelly roll pan with oil then set your oven to 450 degrees before doing anything else.
- Get bowl, combine: cayenne, flour, chili powder, paprika, black pepper, and salt.
- Get a 2nd bowl, combine: milk and eggs. Whisk everything together evenly. Then evenly coat your potatoes with the egg mix then the dry mix.
- Place everything on the jelly roll pan then top the wedges with the veggie oil evenly.
- Cook everything in the oven for about 22 to 26 mins.
- Enjoy.

Amount per serving 6

Timing Information:

Preparation	15 m
Cooking	20 m
Total Time	35 m

Nutritional Information:

Calories	10.8 g
Fat	62.4g
Carbohydrates	9.2 g
Protein	32 mg
Cholesterol	421 mg
Sodium	10.8 g

* Percent Daily Values are based on a 2,000 calorie diet.

NEW JERSEY DINER STYLE FRIES

INGREDIENTS

- 1 large baking potato, cut into wedges
- 1 tablespoon olive oil
- 1/2 teaspoon paprika
- 1/2 tsp Italian seasoning
- 1/2 teaspoon garlic powder
- 1/2 teaspoon chili powder
- 1/2 teaspoon onion powder

Directions

- Set your oven to 450 degrees before doing anything else.
- Get a bowl for your potatoes and combine with them: onion powder, olive oil, chili powder, garlic powder, Italian spice, and paprika.
- Lay our wedges on a baking sheet that has been coated with non-stick spray then cook everything in the oven for 40 to 46 mins.
- Enjoy.

Amount per serving 1

Timing Information:

Preparation	5 m
Cooking	45 m
Total Time	50 m

Nutritional Information:

Calories	357 kcal
Fat	14.1 g
Carbohydrates	54.7g
Protein	5.4 g
Cholesterol	0 mg
Sodium	27 mg

* Percent Daily Values are based on a 2,000 calorie diet.

FRENCH FRY DINNER BAKE

INGREDIENTS

- 1 tablespoon vegetable oil
- 1 1/2 pounds lean ground beef
- 1/2 onion, diced
- 1/2 green bell pepper, diced
- salt and black pepper to taste
- 1 10.75 ounce can condensed cream of mushroom soup
- 3/4 cup processed cheese sauce such as Cheez Whiz
- 1/2 28 ounce package frozen shoestring potato fries

Directions

- Coat a casserole dish with oil then set your oven to 400 degrees before doing anything else.
- As the oven heats begin to fry your ground beef in oil then combine in the green pepper and onion. Stir fry the beef for 14 mins until it is fully done. Add some pepper and salt then combine in the soup. Stir everything together, then get the mix simmering. Once everything is gently boiling, set the heat to low.
- Place your cheese in the microwave for about 45 secs to melt down then layer the beef into the casserole dish. Top the beef with the cheese then layer your fries over everything.
- Cook the dish in the oven for 20 mins or until everything the fries are finished.
- Enjoy.

Amount per serving 6

Timing Information:

Preparation	10 m
Cooking	40 m
Total Time	50 m

Nutritional Information:

Calories	476 kcal
Fat	29 g
Carbohydrates	24.9g
Protein	28 g
Cholesterol	99 mg
Sodium	31214 mg

* Percent Daily Values are based on a 2,000 calorie diet.

FRENCH FRIES FOREVER

INGREDIENTS

- 4 large russet potatoes, peeled and cut into 1/4 inch thick fries
- 1/4 cup vegetable oil
- 1/4 cup tomato-vegetable juice cocktail
- 1 tablespoon chili powder
- 1 teaspoon ground cumin
- 2 teaspoons dried onion granules
- 1 teaspoon garlic powder
- 1 teaspoon cayenne pepper
- 1 teaspoon white sugar
- 1 tablespoon salt

Directions

- Coat a jelly roll pan with oil then set your oven to 375 degrees before doing anything else.
- Get bowl, combine: potatoes, and cold water. Let them sit submerged for 20 mins.
- Get a 2nd bowl, combine: salt, oil, sugar, tomato juice, cayenne, chili powder, garlic powder, onion, and cumin.
- Remove your potatoes from the water then dry them with some towels then place them in the powder and oil mix. Toss everything to evenly top the potatoes with spice mix then place everything into the jelly roll pan.
- Cook the fries in the oven for 25 mins then flip the potatoes and continue cooking for about another 15 mins.
- Enjoy.

Amount per serving 4

Timing Information:

Preparation	10 m
Cooking	40 m
Total Time	50 m

Nutritional Information:

Calories	427 kcal
Fat	14.5 g
Carbohydrates	69.1g
Protein	8.2 g
Cholesterol	0 mg
Sodium	1827 mg

* Percent Daily Values are based on a 2,000 calorie diet.

Simple Portuguese Inspired Fries

INGREDIENTS

- 1 quart oil for frying
- 3 large potatoes, julienned
- 3 cups chopped fresh cilantro
- salt and pepper to taste

Directions

- Get your oil hot to about 350 degrees in a Dutch oven.
- Working in batches cook about one third of the potatoes in the oil for about 6 mins. Then add in the cilantro and continue cooking them for 60 more secs. Place the potatoes to the side on some paper towel lined plates.
- Continue frying potatoes in batches like this and draining them. After all the potatoes have been fried and drain top them with some pepper and salt.
- Enjoy.

Amount per serving 6

Timing Information:

Preparation	30 m
Cooking	30 m
Total Time	1 h

Nutritional Information:

Calories	277 kcal
Fat	15 g
Carbohydrates	33.1g
Protein	4.2 g
Cholesterol	0 mg
Sodium	409 mg

* Percent Daily Values are based on a 2,000 calorie diet.

ELEGANT TRUFFLE OIL AND PARSLEY FRIES

INGREDIENTS

- cooking spray
- 1 pound potatoes, cut into strips - or more to taste
- salt and ground black pepper to taste
- 1 tablespoon white truffle oil, or to taste
- 2 teaspoons chopped fresh parsley, or more to taste

Directions

- Coat a jelly roll pan with non-stick spray then set your oven to 350 degrees before doing anything else.
- Layer your potato on the jelly roll pan and top them with a bit nonstick spray. Toss the potatoes then top them with some pepper and salt and toss everything again.
- Cook the potatoes in the oven for 35 mins then let them loose their heat. Place everything into a bowl and coat the potatoes evenly with more salt, parsley, and truffle oil. Stir the potatoes to evenly coat them with oil and spice.
- Enjoy.

Amount per serving 4

Timing Information:

Preparation	15 m
Cooking	30 m
Total Time	50 m

Nutritional Information:

Calories	120 kcal
Fat	3.7 g
Carbohydrates	19.9g
Protein	2.3 g
Cholesterol	0 mg
Sodium	7 mg

* Percent Daily Values are based on a 2,000 calorie diet.

How to Bake French Fries

INGREDIENTS

- cooking spray
- 2 large potatoes, cut into 1/4-inch slices
- 2 tablespoons vegetable oil
- 1/4 cup grated Parmesan cheese
- 1 tablespoon garlic powder
- 1 tablespoon chopped fresh basil
- 1 tablespoon salt
- 1 tablespoon coarsely ground black pepper

Directions

- Set your oven to 375 degrees before doing anything else.
- Get a casserole dish and cover it with foil. Coat the foil with some nonstick spray then place your potatoes in a bowl.
- Cover your potatoes with veggie oil and toss them then combine in the black pepper, parmesan, salt, basil, and garlic powder. Toss everything again to evenly coat the potatoes then layer them into the casserole dish evenly.
- Cook everything in the oven for 31 to 36 mins or until the fries are golden.
- Enjoy.

Amount per serving 4

Timing Information:

Preparation	10 m
Cooking	30 m
Total Time	40 m

Nutritional Information:

Calories	236 kcal
Fat	8.5 g
Carbohydrates	35g
Protein	6.2 g
Cholesterol	4 mg
Sodium	1833 mg

* Percent Daily Values are based on a 2,000 calorie diet.

LOUISIANA CREOLE FRIES

INGREDIENTS

- 1/4 cup olive oil
- 1 teaspoon garlic powder
- 1 teaspoon onion powder
- 1 teaspoon chili powder
- 1 teaspoon Cajun/Creole seasoning, see appendix
- 1 teaspoon sea salt
- 6 large baking potatoes, sliced into thin wedges

Directions

- Set your oven to 400 degrees before doing anything else.
- Get a bowl, combine: sea salt, olive oil, Cajun/creole spice, garlic powder, chili powder, and onion powder. Stir the spice together evenly then combine in the potatoes.
- Toss everything together evenly then layer it all in a casserole dish spaced out evenly.
- Cook the fries in the oven for about 30 to 37 mins then flip the potatoes and continue bake them for 8 more mins.
- Enjoy.

Amount per serving 6

Timing Information:

Preparation	15 m
Cooking	45 m
Total Time	1 h

Nutritional Information:

Calories	369 kcal
Fat	9.4 g
Carbohydrates	65.5g
Protein	7.7 g
Cholesterol	0 mg
Sodium	399 mg

* Percent Daily Values are based on a 2,000 calorie diet

EASY AZTEC STYLE FRIES

INGREDIENTS

- 2 pounds yucca, peeled, and cut into 4 inch sections
- 2 quarts vegetable oil for frying
- salt to taste

Directions

- Get your yucca boiling in a saucepan. Once the mix is boiling place a lid on the pot, set the heat to low and let gently boil for 25 mins. Remove the liquid then slice the yucca into matchsticks when they have cool off enough to be handled easily.
- Remember to discard the hard inner center of the yuccas.
- Begin to get your oil hot to about 350 to 370 degrees then once the oil is hot working in sets fry about 1/3 to 1/4 of the fries for about 6 to 7 mins per set.
- Lay your yucca fries out to drain then once everything is cool top them with salt.
- Enjoy.

Amount per serving 6

Timing Information:

Preparation	15 m
Cooking	35 m
Total Time	1 h

Nutritional Information:

Calories	437 kcal
Fat	29.3 g
Carbohydrates	40.9g
Protein	5.3 g
Cholesterol	0 mg
Sodium	73 mg

* Percent Daily Values are based on a 2,000 calorie diet.

INDIAN STYLE CURRY CUMIN FRIES

INGREDIENTS

- 1 russet potato, cut into evenly sized strips
- 1 quart vegetable oil for frying
- 1/4 tsp curry powder
- 1/4 tsp cumin
- salt to taste

Directions

- Let your potato sit submerged in water for 45 mins. Then drain and dry them evenly.
- Get your oil hot in a Dutch oven to about 270 to 275 degrees then fry the potatoes for 6 mins in the hot oil for 2 mins then flip the fries and fry them for about 2 to 3 mins. Place the fries on a paper towel lined plate to drain and continue frying everything in batches.
- Once all the fries have been cooked increase the temperature of the oil to 350 degrees and working in batched re-fry your potatoes for 4 to 5 mins then place them to the side again to drain.
- Place all the fries into a bowl then top them with cumin, curry, and salt and toss everything completely and evenly.
- Enjoy.

Amount per serving 2

Timing Information:

Preparation	10 m
Cooking	10 m
Total Time	50 m

Nutritional Information:

Calories	437 kcal
Fat	29.3 g
Carbohydrates	40.9g
Protein	5.3 g
Cholesterol	0 mg
Sodium	73 mg

* Percent Daily Values are based on a 2,000 calorie diet.

SUMMER SAFFLOWER FRIES

INGREDIENTS

- cooking spray
- 6 Yukon Gold potatoes, cut into thick fries
- 1 tablespoon white sugar
- 1/4 cup Safflower oil
- 1 tsp tarragon
- 1 teaspoon garlic powder, or more to taste
- 1 teaspoon salt, or more to taste
- 1 teaspoon ground black pepper, or more to taste

Directions

- Cover a casserole dish with foil the coat the foil with nonstick spray then set your oven to 425 degrees before doing anything else.
- Get a colander for your potatoes and top them with the sugar evenly and toss. Let the potatoes sit for 40 mins to drain.
- Get a bowl, combine: black pepper, tarragon, potatoes, Safflower oil, salt, and garlic powder.
- Toss the potatoes evenly in the oil then layer them in the casserole dish evenly.
- Cook everything in the oven for 25 mins then turn the fires and continue baking them for about 15 mins.
- Enjoy.

Amount per serving 4

Timing Information:

Preparation	10 m
Cooking	40 m
Total Time	1 h 10 m

Nutritional Information:

Calories	388 kcal
Fat	14.4 g
Carbohydrates	59.8g
Protein	6.6 g
Cholesterol	0 mg
Sodium	601 mg

* Percent Daily Values are based on a 2,000 calorie diet.

COUNTRY CILANTRO BASIL RUSTIC SWEET POTATO FRIES

INGREDIENTS

- 2 sweet potatoes, cut into French fries
- 1 tablespoon olive oil
- 1/4 cup Parmesan cheese
- 2 tablespoons chopped fresh cilantro
- 1 tbsp fresh basil, chopped
- sea salt and ground black pepper to taste

Directions

- Set your oven to 425 degrees before doing anything else.
- Get bowl, combine: olive oil, and sweet potatoes. Stir everything completely then layer the potatoes in a casserole dish.
- Cook the fries in the oven for 14 mins then then flip them and continue to cooking them for about another 10 mins.
- Place everything into a serving bowl and top the fries, while they are still hot with the parmesan, basil, and cilantro. Toss everything then add the salt, toss again then add the pepper.
- Enjoy.

Amount per serving 2

Timing Information:

Preparation	15 m
Cooking	20 m
Total Time	35 m

Nutritional Information:

Calories	299 kcal
Fat	9.7 g
Carbohydrates	46.2g
Protein	7.5 g
Cholesterol	9 mg
Sodium	439 mg

* Percent Daily Values are based on a 2,000 calorie diet.

July 4th Mustard Pepper Lime Fries

INGREDIENTS

- 4 russet potatoes, peeled and cut into 1/4 inch thick fries
- 3 tablespoons olive oil
- 2 tablespoons lime juice
- 2 cloves garlic, minced
- 1/2 teaspoon red pepper flakes
- 1/4 teaspoon cayenne pepper
- 1 teaspoon chili powder
- 2 tablespoons spicy brown mustard
- 1/2 teaspoon ground black pepper
- 1 teaspoon salt

Directions

- Set your oven to 400 degrees before doing anything else.
- Get a bowl, combine: pepper, olive oil, mustard, lime juice, chili powder, and garlic, cayenne, and pepper flakes. Stir the spices then add in the potatoes and toss everything nicely.
- Place the fries in a jelly roll pan that has been greased lightly or coated with non-stick spray and cook everything in the oven for 18 mins. Flip the potatoes and continue cooking for 14 more mins or until the potatoes are completely done.
- Enjoy after topping the fries with salt.

Amount per serving 4

Timing Information:

Preparation	10 m
Cooking	30 m
Total Time	40 m

Nutritional Information:

Calories	269 kcal
Fat	11 g
Carbohydrates	39.6g
Protein	5 g
Cholesterol	0 mg
Sodium	699 mg

* Percent Daily Values are based on a 2,000 calorie diet.

BUTTER LEMON PEPPER FRENCH FRIES

INGREDIENTS

- 1 32 ounce package frozen French fries
- 2 1/2 tablespoons lemon pepper
- 2 tablespoons dried red pepper seasoning
- 1 tablespoon garlic powder
- black pepper to taste
- 2 pinches chili powder
- 1/4 cup butter

Directions

- Set your oven to 425 degrees before doing anything else.
- Coat a baking dish with some nonstick spray then place your potatoes in the dish. Top the potatoes with: chili powder, lemon pepper, garlic powder, red pepper. Toss everything then dot the fries with the butter evenly.
- Cook everything in the oven for 17 mins flipping the potatoes half way. If the fries are not done cook them for about 7 more mins.
- Enjoy.

Amount per serving 8

Timing Information:

Preparation	10 m
Cooking	20 m
Total Time	30 m

Nutritional Information:

Calories	227 kcal
Fat	11.3 g
Carbohydrates	29.9g
Protein	3 g
Cholesterol	15 mg
Sodium	849 mg

* Percent Daily Values are based on a 2,000 calorie diet.

COPYCAT FAST FOOD FRANCHISE FRIES

INGREDIENTS

- 8 potatoes, peeled and cut into 1/4-inch thick fries
- 1/4 cup white sugar
- 2 tablespoons corn syrup
- 1 quart canola oil, or as needed
- boiling water
- sea salt to taste

Directions

- Get a bowl, for your potatoes and let them sit submerged in water for 15 mins then remove the liquid and dry the potatoes.
- Now submerge the potatoes in just enough boiling water then add in the corn syrup and sugar and stir everything. Do this in a metal bowl. Put everything in the fridge for 10 mins. Remove the liquid and dry the potatoes with some paper towels.
- Get a casserole dish or jelly roll pan and lay out the fries on the dish, place a covering plastic on the dish and put everything in the freezer for 45 mins.
- Now get your oil hot for frying to about 350 to 360 degrees and once the oil is hot begin to 1.3 of the fries in the oil for 3 mins. Place the fries on a plate with some paper towel to drain and let them for about 10 mins. Continue to work in batches until all the fries are done.
- Now re fry the fries a second time 1/3 at a time for 6 mins each batch then season the fries with some salt.
- Enjoy.

Amount per serving 4

Timing Information:

Preparation	10 m
Cooking	10 m
Total Time	1 h 15 m

Nutritional Information:

Calories	600 kcal
Fat	322.4 g
Carbohydrates	394.8g
Protein	38.6 g
Cholesterol	0 mg
Sodium	112 mg

* Percent Daily Values are based on a 2,000 calorie diet.

FRENCH SEASONED FRIES WITH TOURTIERE

INGREDIENTS

- 2 1/2 pounds russet potatoes, peeled, cut into matchsticks, soaked in cold water
- 1 cup all-purpose flour
- 1 teaspoon garlic salt
- 1 teaspoon onion salt
- 1 tsp Tourtiere spice mix, see appendix
- 1 teaspoon salt
- 1 teaspoon paprika
- 1/2 cup water, or as needed
- 1 cup vegetable oil for frying

Directions

- Get your oil hot in a frying pan.
- As the oil heats begin to sift the following spices into a bowl: paprika, Tourtiere, flour, salt, garlic salt, and onion salt. Add in a small amount of water to make the spice mix slightly battery just enough so that it would drip from a utensils.
- Coat your fries evenly with batter carefully then carefully place them into the hot oil. Make sure you lay each fry into the oil separately so as to avoid any sticking together.
- Let the fry cook until they are golden.

Amount per serving 8

Timing Information:

Preparation	Enjoy.
Cooking	
Total Time	15 m

Nutritional Information:

Calories	192 kcal
Fat	3.1 g
Carbohydrates	37.8g
Protein	3.9 g
Cholesterol	0 mg
Sodium	751 mg

* Percent Daily Values are based on a 2,000 calorie diet.

LOADED STATE FAIR FRIES

INGREDIENTS

- 1 32 ounce package frozen seasoned French fries
- 2 tablespoons cornstarch
- 2 tablespoons water
- 2 cups low-fat milk
- 1 tablespoon margarine
- 8 slices American cheese, cut into pieces
- 1 15 ounce can chili without beans such as Hormel, or vegetarian chili for meatless

Directions

- Cook your fries in the oven for about 25 mins until they are golden brown at 350 degrees.
- Get a small bowl and combine your water and cornstarch evenly.
- Get a saucepan with the margarine and milk boiling while whisking then set the heat to low and stir in the cornstarch mix into the milk mix. Set the heat to a medium level and continue heat the mix until it becomes thick while stirring.
- Combine in the cheese slices and stir the mix until everything is melted. Then heat your chili in a separate pot.
- Once the milk mix is done and the chili as well top your fries with the chili and cheese and serve.
- Enjoy.

Amount per serving 6

Timing Information:

Preparation	5 m
Cooking	20 m
Total Time	25 m

Nutritional Information:

Calories	509 kcal
Fat	25.2 g
Carbohydrates	351.6g
Protein	19.8 g
Cholesterol	449 mg
Sodium	1484 mg

* Percent Daily Values are based on a 2,000 calorie diet.

RUSTIC WINDMILL FRIES

INGREDIENTS

- 4 medium Yukon Gold potatoes, wedges
- 1 tablespoon butter
- 1 tablespoon olive oil, or more to taste
- 2 cloves garlic, minced
- 1/2 teaspoon Fine Sea Salt
- 1 teaspoon ground black pepper

Directions

- Set your oven to 400 degrees before doing anything else.
- Get your garlic, olive oil, and butter heating in a pot then combine in the salt and pepper. Stir everything evenly then coat the wedges evenly with the garlic sauce.
- Place everything into a casserole dish evenly dispersed and for 40 mins cook the fries in the oven.
- Enjoy.

Amount per serving 2

Timing Information:

Preparation	20 m
Cooking	30 m
Total Time	50 m

Nutritional Information:

Calories	310 kcal
Fat	12.8 g
Carbohydrates	45.5g
Protein	5.4 g
Cholesterol	15 mg
Sodium	497 mg

* Percent Daily Values are based on a 2,000 calorie diet.

SAINT FRANCIS'S FEAST FRIES

INGREDIENTS

- olive oil cooking spray
- 4 russet potatoes
- 1 tablespoon olive oil
- 1 tablespoon chopped fresh rosemary
- 1 1/2 teaspoons dried thyme leaves
- 1 teaspoon garlic powder
- 1/2 teaspoon dried oregano leaves
- 1/2 teaspoon dried parsley
- 1/2 teaspoon ground sage
- 1/2 teaspoon cracked black pepper
- 1/4 teaspoon salt

Directions

- Coat a casserole dish or jelly roll pan with nonstick spray then set your oven to 425 degrees before doing anything else.
- Get a bowl for your potatoes and place a towel over the bowl or some plastic wrap and cook everything in the microwave for 5 mins with a high level of heat. Let the potatoes lose their heat then slice each one into wedges.
- Get a 2nd bowl for your cut potatoes and coat them with the olive oil and toss them. Layer the potatoes on the jelly roll pan or casserole dish and cook them with the oven for 12 mins then coat them some nonstick spray and cook them for 14 more mins.
- Get a small dish and combine: salt, rosemary, pepper, thyme, sage, parsley, garlic powder, and oregano.
- Top your potatoes with the spice mix while they are still hot and toss them.
- Enjoy.

Amount per serving 4

Timing Information:

Preparation	5 m
Cooking	25 m
Total Time	30 m

Nutritional Information:

Calories	99 kcal
Fat	3.6 g
Carbohydrates	15.9g
Protein	1.6 g
Cholesterol	0 mg
Sodium	153 mg

* Percent Daily Values are based on a 2,000 calorie diet.

VISHNU'S DELIGHT FRIES

INGREDIENTS

- 6 potatoes, cut into wedges
- 2 tablespoons vegetable oil
- 2 tablespoons shredded Parmesan cheese
- 2 teaspoons curry powder
- 1 teaspoon paprika
- 1 teaspoon salt
- 1/2 teaspoon garlic powder

Directions

- Set your oven to 400 degrees before doing anything else.
- Coat a jelly roll pan with nonstick spray.
- Get a bowl, combine: garlic powder, veggie oil, salt, parmesan, paprika, and curry. Toss everything evenly to coat the potatoes layer everything into the pan.
- Cook the wedges in the oven for about 14 mins then flip them and continue cooking for 10 more mins.
- Enjoy.

Amount per serving 8

Timing Information:

Preparation	10 m
Cooking	20 m
Total Time	30 m

Nutritional Information:

Calories	162 kcal
Fat	4.1 g
Carbohydrates	28.5g
Protein	3.8 g
Cholesterol	< 1 mg
Sodium	< 322 mg

* Percent Daily Values are based on a 2,000 calorie diet.

FRENCH FRIES FOR BREAKFAST

INGREDIENTS

- 1 teaspoon butter, or to taste
- 1/4 cup frozen French fries, or to taste
- 2 eggs, beaten
- 1 pinch salt and ground black pepper to taste

Directions

- Get your butter hot and melted in a cast iron pan. Then once the butter is hot add in your fries and cook them for about 6 mins. Combine in your salt and eggs, then the pepper and continue to stir everything for about 4 to 6 more mins.
- Enjoy.

Amount per serving 1

Timing Information:

Preparation	5 m
Cooking	10 m
Total Time	15 m

Nutritional Information:

Calories	212 kcal
Fat	15.1 g
Carbohydrates	6.4g
Protein	13.1 g
Cholesterol	2383 mg
Sodium	12399 mg

* Percent Daily Values are based on a 2,000 calorie diet.

Curried French Fries from Jamaica

INGREDIENTS

- 2 1/2 pounds russet potatoes, peeled, cut into matchsticks, soaked in cold water
- 1 cup all-purpose flour
- 1 teaspoon garlic salt
- 1 teaspoon onion salt
- 1 tsp Jamaican Curry spice mix, see appendix
- 1 teaspoon salt
- 1 teaspoon paprika
- 1/2 cup water, or as needed
- 1 cup vegetable oil for frying

Directions

- Get your oil hot in a frying pan.
- As the oil heats begin to sift the following spices into a bowl: paprika, Jamaican curry spice mix, flour, salt, garlic salt, and onion salt. Add in a small amount of water to make the spice mix slightly battery just enough so that it would drip from a utensils.
- Coat your fries evenly with batter carefully then carefully place them into the hot oil. Make sure you lay each fry into the oil separately so as to avoid any sticking together.
- Let the fry cook until they are golden.
- Enjoy.

Amount per serving 8

Timing Information:

Preparation	15 m
Cooking	10 m
Total Time	25 m

Nutritional Information:

Calories	192 kcal
Fat	3.1 g
Carbohydrates	37.8g
Protein	3.9 g
Cholesterol	0 mg
Sodium	751 mg

* Percent Daily Values are based on a 2,000 calorie diet.

FRENCH SPICE MIX I (HERBS DE PROVENCE II)

This is a spice mix popular in southern France. It is great in veggie stews and as a dry rub for grilled meats. This spice provides a very unique taste that is characteristic of France.

Ingredients

- 2 tbsps dried rosemary
- 1 tbsp fennel seed
- 2 tbsps dried savory
- 2 tbsps dried thyme
- 2 tbsps dried basil
- 2 tbsps dried marjoram
- 2 tbsps dried lavender flowers
- 2 tbsps dried Italian parsley
- 1 tbsp dried oregano
- 1 tbsp dried tarragon
- 1 tsp bay powder

Directions

- With a mortar and pestle grind fennel seed and rosemary. Then combine with bay powder, savory, fennel, thyme, rosemary, basil, parsley, marjoram, oregano, lavender, and tarragon in a bowl.
- Then transfer to an appropriate container for storage.

Timing Information:

Preparation	Cooking	Total Time
5 m		5 m

Nutritional Information:

Calories	2 kcal
Fat	0 g
Carbohydrates	0.3g
Protein	0.1 g
Cholesterol	0 mg
Sodium	1 mg

* Percent Daily Values are based on a 2,000 calorie diet.

FRENCH SPICE MIX II (TOURTIERE SEASONING)

This is a spice mix popular in Canadian and French cuisines for meats and meat pies. Try it yourself it has a very savory and full flavor.

Ingredients

- 1 tsp celery salt
- 1/2 tsp ground black pepper
- 1/2 tsp crushed savory
- 1/2 tsp ground cloves
- 1/2 tsp ground cinnamon
- 1/2 tsp ground thyme
- 1/4 tsp ground sage
- 1/4 tsp mustard powder

Directions

- Get a bowl sift or mix evenly: mustard powder, celery salt, sage, pepper, thyme, savory, cinnamon, and cloves.
- Get your air tight container and store the dry mix for continued use.

Timing Information:

Preparation	Cooking	Total Time
5 m		5 m

Nutritional Information:

Calories	5 kcal
Fat	0.2 g
Carbohydrates	0.9g
Protein	0.2 g
Cholesterol	0 mg
Sodium	372 mg

* Percent Daily Values are based on a 2,000 calorie diet.

Caribbean Mix II (Jamaican Curry)

Not all curries come out of Asia. This is a Caribbean style one will provide a new and unique taste.

Ingredients

- 1/4 C. whole coriander seeds
- 2 tbsps whole cumin seeds
- 2 tbsps whole mustard seeds
- 2 tbsps whole anise seeds
- 1 tbsp whole fenugreek seeds
- 1 tbsp whole allspice berries
- 5 tbsps ground turmeric

Directions

- Combine the coriander seeds, cumin seeds, mustard seeds, anise seeds, fenugreek seeds, and allspice berries in a skillet.
- Toast over medium heat until the color of the spices slightly darkens, and the spices are very fragrant, about 10 minutes. Remove the spices from the skillet, and allow them to cool to room temperature. Grind the spices with the turmeric in a spice grinder. Store in an airtight container at room temperature.
- Get a frying hot without oil, toast the following for 11 mins: allspice berries, coriander seeds, fenugreek seeds, cumin seeds, anise seeds, and mustard seeds.
- Get a mortar and pestle or your preferred grinder and grind all the toasted spices with turmeric as well.
- Enter everything into your storage containers.

Timing Information:

Preparation	Cooking	Total Time
10 m	11 m	21 m

Nutritional Information:

Calories	12 kcal
Fat	0.5 g
Carbohydrates	1.8g
Protein	0.5 g
Cholesterol	0 mg
Sodium	2 mg

* Percent Daily Values are based on a 2,000 calorie diet.

CAJUN SPICE MIX

This Cajun style seasoning can be used for meats but one of its best uses is for potatoes which you should bake in the oven.

Ingredients

- 2 tsps salt
- 2 tsps garlic powder
- 2 1/2 tsps paprika
- 1 tsp ground black pepper
- 1 tsp onion powder

- 1 tsp cayenne pepper
- 1 1/4 tsps dried oregano
- 1 1/4 tsps dried thyme
- 1/2 tsp red pepper flakes (optional)

Directions

- Get a bowl, evenly mix or sift: red pepper flakes, salt, thyme, garlic powder, oregano, paprika, cayenne, onion powder, and black pepper.
- Get a good container that is airtight and store your mix.

Timing Information:

Preparation	Cooking	Total Time
5 m		5 m

Nutritional Information:

Calories	6 kcal
Fat	0.1 g
Carbohydrates	1.2g
Protein	0.2 g
Cholesterol	0 mg
Sodium	388 mg

* Percent Daily Values are based on a 2,000 calorie diet.

Printed in Great Britain
by Amazon